Classworks

Fiction and Poetry Texts

Julie Orrell

Published in 2004 by:
Nelson Thornes Ltd
Delta Place
27 Bath Road
CHELTENHAM
GL53 7TH
United Kingdom

04 05 06 07 08 / 10 9 8 7 6 5 4 3 2 1

A catalogue record for this book is available from the British Library

ISBN 0-7487-8646-5

Illustrations by Jacqueline East, Woody Fox, Mike Phillips, Nick Schon
and Alex Machin
Page make-up by GreenGate Publishing Services, Tonbridge, Kent

Printed in Great Britain by Ashford Colour Press

Acknowledgements

All texts written by and copyright Julie Orrell except:

Extract from 'The Big Big Sea' written by Martin Waddell, and originally illustrated
by Jennifer Eachus Text Copyright © 1994 Martin Waddell Reproduced by
permission of Walker Books Ltd., London, SE11 5HJ ; 'What Is a Million?'
Copyright © Wes Magee; 'Hector the Collector' from *Where the Sidewalk Ends* by
Shel Silverstein Copyright © 1974 by Evil Eye Music, Inc.; renewed 2002 by Evil
Eye, LLC By permission of Edite Kroll Literary Agency Inc; 'Steel Band Jump Up'
by Faustin Charles from the anthology *A Caribbean Dozen* edited by John Agard
and Grace Nichols, and illustrated by Cathie Felstead Copyright © 1994 Faustin
Charles Reproduced by permission of Walker Books Ltd, London, SE11 5HJ;
'The Pow-wow Drum' by David Campbell from the anthology *A Caribbean Dozen*,
edited by John Agard and Grace Nichols, and illustrated by Cathie Felstead
Copyright © 1994 David Campbell Reproduced by permission of Walker Books
Ltd, London, SE11 5HJ; the editor and publisher thank the following for
permission to reprint 'Snake in School' by Debjani Chatterjee which was first
published in *Poems about School* from Wayland Publishers in 1999; 'A Who'Z Who
of the Horrible House' Copyright © Wes Magee; 'The Witch's Brew' Copyright
© Wes Magee; Extract from 'In the middle of the night' written by Kathy
Henderson and illustrated by Jennifer Eachus Text Copyright © 1992 Kathy
Henderson Reproduced by permission of Walker Books Ltd., London, SE11 5HJ;
Extract from 'The little boat' written by Kathy Henderson and illustrated by Patrick
Benson Text Copyright © 1995 Kathy Henderson Reproduced by permission of
Walker Books Ltd. London, SE11 5HJ; 'Spellbound' by Norman Vandal; 'Sunday in
the Yarm Fard' Copyright © Trevor Millum 1990; *Charlie and the Chocolate Factory*
Copyright © Roald Dahl 1967 reproduced by permission of David Higham
Associates; *James and the Giant Peach* Copyright © Roald Dahl 1967 reproduced
by permission of David Higham Associates

Cover image: #559200 © Walter Bibikow/Index Stock Imagery: Seahorse Statue,
Malecon, Puerta Vallarta, Mexico

Every effort has been made to trace the copyright holders, but if any have been
inadvertently overlooked, the publishers will be pleased to make the necessary
arrangement at the first opportunity.

Contents

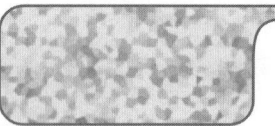

How to use this book

What this book contains	• Extracts from published works, plus tailor-made extracts, all arranged and chosen specifically to match the examples of medium-term planning provided by the National Literacy Strategy
	• Teaching ideas for each extract to get you started, covering some of the relevant text, sentence or word level objectives from the relevant unit
How you can use *Classworks Literacy Texts* with other resources	• The blocked unit structure means you can dip into the book to find resources perfect for what you're teaching this week – it doesn't matter what plan, scheme or other resource you're using
	• There are two *Classworks Literacy Texts* books for every year from Reception (or Primary 1) to Year 6 (or Primary 7): one contains Fiction and Poetry, the other contains Non-fiction. Both books together contain texts for every unit of the medium-term plans

What each page does

Text number

Title of extract

Text (with illustration where appropriate)

Author or origin of text

Unit title (usually a type of text, for example, narrative structure)

Sub-section of unit (for example, story openings)

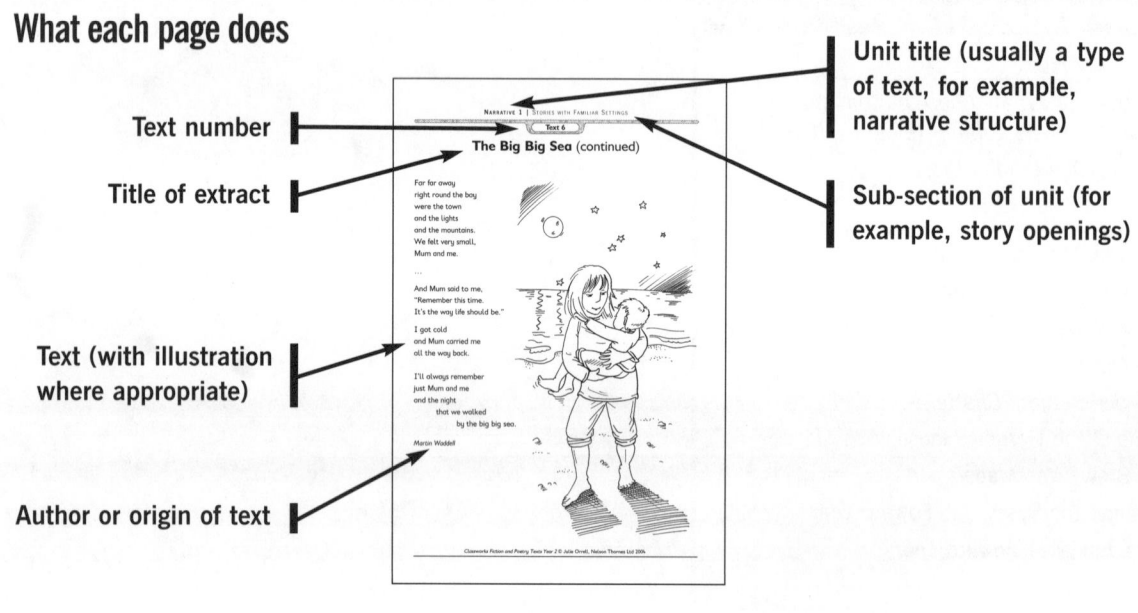

Term

Unit title

Sub-section of unit

Text number

Title of extract

Teaching idea

Relevant Literacy Framework objective

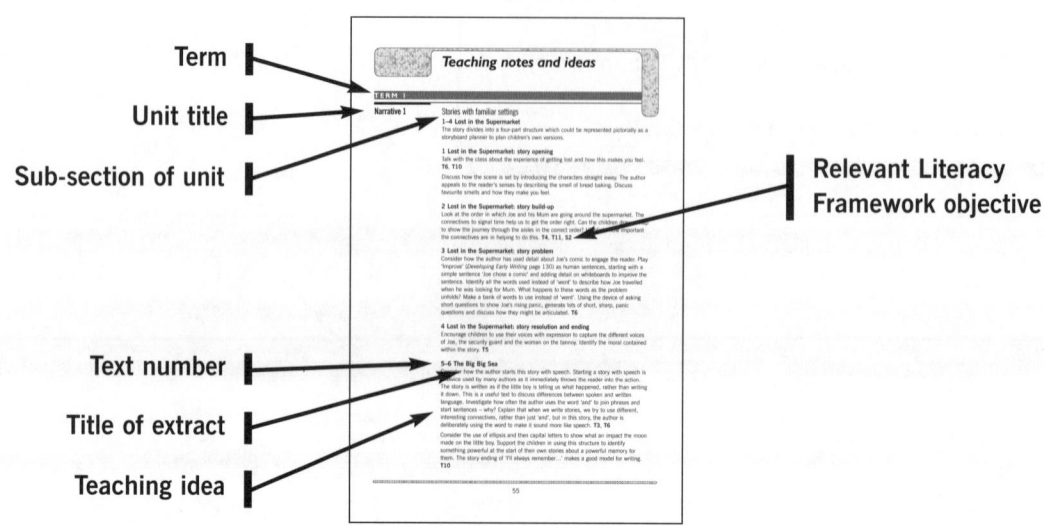

Text 1

Lost in the Supermarket
Story opening

Joe liked to go shopping with his mum. He enjoyed the sights and sounds of the busy supermarket on Saturday mornings. The smells changed as you travelled around the shop: his favourite was the bakery smell of warm bread and hot cross buns.

On this particular Saturday, Joe was looking forward to the trip to the supermarket. Two weeks ago it had been Joe's birthday and he still had some of his birthday money from Granny left, which he was planning to spend on his favourite comic. Joe's mum parked the car and they went in through the sliding doors that seemed to know when you were coming and opened specially for you.

Text 2

Lost in the Supermarket
Story build-up

First they came to the fruit and vegetable stalls. Joe helped Mum choose the rosiest red apples and the greenest grapes. Next, they went past the warm cabinets where delicious smells tempted them to try the tasty bits on cocktail sticks in the little bowls.

The next aisle was full of cheeses and meats in big fridge cabinets. Joe liked to hurry through this one as it always made him feel cold and shivery, but this Saturday his mum took a long time. After a few minutes, Joe left the trolley and wandered over to the newsagent's shelves to have a quick look at the comics. He thought he would catch Mum up again before the bakery.

It was easy to find the comics displayed on the shelves. They were so bright and colourful that they seemed to shout out at you, "Choose me! I've got the best free gift! I've got the biggest poster inside!" The trouble was that Joe wanted to choose the best comic, not just the one that was shouting loudest! One by one, he peeped inside to see which would be the best to buy with his birthday money.

Text 3

Lost in the Supermarket
Story problem

Five minutes later, Joe chose a comic. It was a Spiderman comic, with a free spider's web and suction pads that you could use to stick it onto your window. Clutching his comic, Joe skipped back to find Mum. He went first to the cold aisle, but she was not there any more. He walked next to the aisles of tins and jars, but she was not there either. Finally he walked right on to the bakery – no Mum!

Joe was beginning to feel a bit scared: where could Mum be? He raced back and went along the aisles again, but there was no sign of Mum or the trolley. Mum was nowhere to be found. How could he have lost her? Surely she wouldn't have left without him? What should he do? Joe's heart was beating like a drum.

Suddenly, Joe turned and saw a man in a black uniform coming towards him. Joe started to cry.

Classworks Fiction and Poetry Texts Year 2 © Julie Orrell, Nelson Thornes Ltd 2004

Text 4

Lost in the Supermarket
Story resolution and ending

"Are you lost?" asked the man in the uniform. He was a security guard and had noticed Joe looking upset.

"I can't find Mum… I only went away for a minute and now she isn't here…" stuttered Joe.

The security man was very kind. He took Joe to the helpdesk where the woman spoke into a loud speaker so that everybody in the supermarket could hear her.

"We have a lost child in the store. His name is Joe and he is waiting at the helpdesk for his mother to collect him. Thank you."

Two minutes later Mum appeared, looking very worried. She had realised that Joe was missing, but had gone a different way as he ran back through the aisles. Mum gave Joe a big hug. Then she took Joe to the café for a drink and a biscuit before they went home. Joe had learnt a lesson: he promised that he would always make sure that Mum knew where he was in future.

Classworks Fiction and Poetry Texts Year 2 © Julie Orrell, Nelson Thornes Ltd 2004

Text 5

The Big Big Sea

Mum said, "Let's go!"
So we went
     out of the house
         and into the dark
            and I saw…

THE MOON.

…

And I ran
and Mum ran.
We ran and we ran
straight through
the puddles
and out to the sea!

I went right in
to the shiny bit.
There was only me
in the big big sea.

…

The Big Big Sea (continued)

Far far away
right round the bay
were the town
and the lights
and the mountains.
We felt very small,
Mum and me.

…

And Mum said to me,
"Remember this time.
It's the way life should be."

I got cold
and Mum carried me
all the way back.

I'll always remember
just Mum and me
and the night
    that we walked
        by the big big sea.

Martin Waddell

Text 7

What Is a Million?

The blades of grass growing
on your back lawn.
The people you've met
since the day you were born.

The age of a fossil
you found by the sea.
The years it would take you
to reach Octran Three.

The water drops needed
to fill the fish pool.
The words you have read
since you started school.

Wes Magee

Text 8

Back to School

Summer's over –
Back to school,
A new class,
New rules.
New teacher,
Seems OK,
New playground
Games to play.
New haircut,
New shoes,
Different toys
And books to choose.
One year older,
School's just fine but…
Further back
In the dinner line!

Text 9

Playground Rap

We like to slide, we like to hide,
It's a playground rap, a playground rap.
We like to sing, we like to swing,
It's a playground rap, a playground rap.
We like to shout, and chase about,
It's a playground rap, a playground rap.
We like to run, we're having fun,
It's a playground rap, a playground rap.
We're in the sun, and school is done,
It's a playground rap, a playground rap! Yeh!

Classworks Fiction and Poetry Texts Year 2 © Julie Orrell, Nelson Thornes Ltd 2004

The Monster in my Bedroom

The monster in my bedroom,
It snores and grunts at night,
Its teeth are sharp as razors
And it's not afraid to bite!

It hides in dusty corners,
It sneaks behind the door,
Its mouth is like a cavern
And it has a fearsome roar!

The monster in my bedroom,
Is very nearly three,
Mum says he is my brother,
And he shares a room with me!

Classworks Fiction and Poetry Texts Year 2 © Julie Orrell, Nelson Thornes Ltd 2004

Hector the Collector

Hector the Collector
Collected bits of string,
Collected dolls with broken heads
And rusty bells that would not ring.
Pieces out of picture puzzles,
Bent-up nails and ice-cream sticks,
Twists of wires, worn-out tyres,
Paper bags and broken bricks.
Old chipped vases, half shoelaces,
Gatlin' guns that wouldn't shoot,
Leaky boats that wouldn't float
And stopped-up horns that wouldn't toot.
Butter knives that had no handles,
Copper keys that fit no locks,
Rings that were too small for fingers,
Dried-up leaves and patched-up socks.
Worn-out belts that had no buckles,
'Lectric trains that had no tracks,
Airplane models, broken bottles,
Three-legged chairs and cups with cracks.
Hector the Collector
Loved these things with all his soul –
Loved them more than shining diamonds,
Loved them more than glistenin' gold.
Hector called to all the people,
"Come and share my treasure trunk!"
And all the silly sightless people
Came and looked... and called it junk.

Shel Silverstein

The First Day of the Holidays
Story opening

It was the first day of the holidays, and the seaside sky was blue and clear.

THE FIRST DAY OF THE HOLIDAYS!

Tegan and Sam could hardly wait to pull on their beach clothes, open the weather-beaten, white-painted door of Gran's cottage and run the few steps to the cove. Tegan felt excitement building up inside her like steam in a kettle, until it grew too much to keep in.

After calling to Gran and grabbing her rucksack, she was off – spilling out of the cottage like the steam finally escaping.

The First Day of the Holidays
Story build-up

A few minutes later, Gran and Sam joined her on the sandy path down to the beach. Gran had packed a picnic of all the sorts of things you dream of when you are at the seaside. After a short while, they reached the beach and Gran set up a special corner for them, using a brightly striped windbreak as a wall.

All morning, the children played in the sand, making sand shapes, collecting shells and trying to dig down deep enough to reach water for a moat. Later, Gran called Sam and Tegan back to the windbreak and they shared a delicious picnic.

Classworks Fiction and Poetry Texts Year 2 © Julie Orrell, Nelson Thornes Ltd 2004

Text 14

The First Day of the Holidays
Story problem

It was late in the afternoon and the children were busy collecting large pebbles and rocks for the dam they were building across the little river that ran down the beach.

They were so busy that at first they did not notice that they had wandered off to another part of the beach, far away from the safety of Gran and the striped windbreak. It was Sam who realised that they were lost. It was Sam who had tears welling up in his eyes as he scanned the beach for Gran.

What could they do? The two children wandered backwards and forwards amongst the windbreaks, feeling more and more afraid. They could see lots of striped windbreaks, but they all looked the same. Which one was Gran's?

Suddenly, Tegan felt a hand on her shoulder...

Text 15

The First Day of the Holidays
Story resolution and ending

She turned and saw that it was the hand of a lifeguard who had been watching them searching the windbreaks for Gran.

"Are you lost?" he asked. Holding each child gently by the hand, he took them back to the lifeguard's hut where a very worried Gran was waiting.

Then, all too soon, it was time to collect up their things and clamber back up the sandy path to where the little cottage waited for them. Tomorrow they would stay closer to Gran!

Classworks Fiction and Poetry Texts Year 2 © Julie Orrell, Nelson Thornes Ltd 2004

The Whisp of Straw, the Piece of Coal and the Little Bean

Story opening

Long, long ago and in a village not far from where you are sitting today, there lived a poor old woman. She lived all alone in a tumbledown cottage and had little to eat. One evening, she went to the stone hearth to light a fire to boil water for her supper. The coal was damp, so the old woman used a handful of straw to get the fire going. All the old woman had for supper was a bowlful of bouncy broad beans. Carefully, she tipped the beans into the boiling water, but as she tipped, one bean bounced out of the pot and down onto the flagstone floor. It landed by a whisp of straw that had fallen as the old woman was lighting the fire.

A while later, a piece of coal fell from the grate and rolled to join the bean and the straw on the floor.

Classworks Fiction and Poetry Texts Year 2 © Julie Orrell, Nelson Thornes Ltd 2004

Text 17

The Whisp of Straw, the Piece of Coal and the Little Bean

Story build-up

The whisp of straw started to talk to his new companions.

"Good day, my friends," he said. "Do tell me, what has brought you here?"

"Well, my friends," answered the coal, "by good chance, I jumped out of the fire. My brothers and sisters have all been burnt to cinders, but I am the lucky one, for I have escaped."

"Well, my friends," answered the bean, "I too have had the best of luck today. If I had ended up in that pot I would have been boiled and eaten like my brothers and sisters."

"Well, my friends," replied the straw, "we have all tricked fate today. For if I had not slipped from the old woman's grasp, I would surely have gone up in flames like my brothers and sisters."

The three companions decided that since they had escaped such terrible fates, they would leave straight away and seek their fortune in the wide world.

Classworks Fiction and Poetry Texts Year 2 © Julie Orell, Nelson Thornes Ltd 2004

Text 18

The Whisp of Straw, the Piece of Coal and the Little Bean
Story problem

Before long, they came to a stream. The three companions had no bridge to help them cross so they pondered how they might cross the river.

After a while, the piece of straw suggested, "Well, my friends. I have a plan. I will lie down across the stream and you, my friends, can use me as a bridge."

Next the straw lay down and just stretched from one bank of the stream to the other. The lump of coal rushed onto the straw bridge but when he was halfway over he stopped, for hot coal fears cold water. The lump of coal was so terrified at the sight of the rushing stream below him that he was too scared to move.

With a crackling sound, the straw caught alight and snapped in two, falling into the water. Without the bridge, the coal, too, slipped sizzling into the stream.

Meanwhile, the bean had sat watching on the side of the bank. He couldn't stop laughing when he saw what happened. I'm sorry to say, he laughed so long and so loud that he burst out of his skin.

Classworks Fiction and Poetry Texts Year 2 © Julie Orrell, Nelson Thornes Ltd 2004

The Whisp of Straw, the Piece of Coal and the Little Bean

Story resolution and ending

And that would have been the end of the tale, but for the good fortune of the bean. A tailor was travelling by and, it being a hot day, had stopped to rest awhile by the stream. The tailor saw the bean and asked his story. The tailor was a kind-hearted man and he took pity on the bean. Fetching a needle and thread from his basket, he sewed the bean up again with a neat seam of stitches. The bean was very grateful and continued on his journey.

And that is the end of the tale, save to say that to this day, broad beans have a black seam as a reminder of the story of the whisp of straw, the piece of coal and the bean.

The Wishing Stone
Story opening

Once upon a time, and not so very far from where you are sitting today, lived an old farmer named Matt. His face was worn, wrinkled and whiskery and his hands were as grained as the leather on an old pair of boots. He lived in an old granite farmhouse, snug beneath a thatched roof.

Matt loved the countryside and knew every fold in the hillsides and every stone on the moors. He had farmed there all his life, as had his father and grandfather before him. He loved to walk the fields and moors with his dog, feeling the hot summer sun on his back and the cool breeze on his wrinkled face. But as for the people of the land – well, that was a different kettle of fish.

For Matt was a selfish man. He kept himself to himself and cared little for his neighbours in their time of need. When the crops failed and there was little to eat in the village, Matt closed his door and said to himself, "No matter, for I have plenty to eat from what my farm provides."

Text 21

The Wishing Stone
Story build-up

One morning, just as the sun was slipping out from the shadows behind the corn, Matt set off on his morning walk with his dog, Jake, at his side. He walked the grassy pathways wet with dew, and smelt the fresh-cut hay in the fields. It must have been a sudden shaft of sunlight that caused Matt to stumble, for when he opened his eyes in the undergrowth of fern, he felt as if he had slept for a thousand years. Ahead of him was a stone, a stone that he had never seen before.

It was old and smooth, round as an eye with a hole for its eyeball, and as tall as Matt himself.

"Well I never," said Matt, reaching forward and touching the stone to check that it was real. He had heard tell of stones hereabouts that had magical powers, stones that a person must climb through three times and three magic wishes would rub off on him. But surely that was just folklore, tales told by the firelight and to children in their beds.

Slowly, he climbed through the hole in the stone. Once, twice, three times. As he climbed through the hole the third time, the dog whined as if he sensed the magic in the air.

Classworks Fiction and Poetry Texts Year 2 © Julie Orrell, Nelson Thornes Ltd 2004

The Wishing stone
Story problem

Matt sat himself down on a hillock of grass and shouted aloud to the westerly wind, "I wish I had a sack of gold!" At that instant, behind his back, he felt something big and bulky that had not been there when he sat down. GOLD!

"I wish I had ten sacks of gold!"

Sure enough, ten sacks of gold appeared beside the first. Matt could hardly believe his eyes; could hardly believe his luck.

"I wish I had a hundred sacks of gold!"

There sat Matt, encircled by sacks of gold, too heavy for two men apiece to lift.

And therein lay the problem. For as soon as Matt set off back to his farm for a wheelbarrow, the magic of the stone closed around it again, hiding it once more in the undergrowth.

Classworks Fiction and Poetry Texts Year 2 © Julie Orrell, Nelson Thornes Ltd 2004

Text 23

The Wishing Stone
Story resolution and ending

Matt never found that stone again, nor did he find the hundred sacks of gold. In the days that followed, Matt began to realise that a hundred sacks of gold are worthless, if you have no one to help you carry them.

The next time the crops failed in the rock-strewn fields, old Matt was there to help those with little to eat. People from the farms and villages would find gifts of turnips and potatoes, milk and honey on the granite doorsteps of their homes. Old men of the village started to seek him out and would walk along the grassy tracks to his farm to pass the time of day, or to help him in the fields.

As the years passed, Matt understood that the wishing stone had given him more than he had asked for. It had given him friends.

Classworks Fiction and Poetry Texts Year 2 © Julie Orrell, Nelson Thornes Ltd 2004

Steel Band Jump Up

I put my ear to the ground,
And I hear the steel-band sound:
Ping pong! Ping pong!
Music deep, rhythm sweet,
I'm dancing tracking the beat;
Like a seashell's ringing song,
Ping pong! Ping pong!
Moving along, moving along,
High and low, up and down,
Ping pong! Ping pong!
Pan beating singing, round and round,
Ping pong! Ping pong!

Faustin Charles

Text 25

The Pow-wow Drum

Long black braids and silken shawls
Moving side by side where the eagle calls,
Answering the beat of the pow-wow drum
we come again
to dance again

Hey-a, Hey-a, Hey-a, Hey-a, Hey!
Hey-a, Hey-a, Hey-a, Hey-a, Hey!

Leave the dusty cities far behind,
Meet our brothers of the country with one mind,
Travelling from the east, north, south and west
we come again
to dance again

Chorus

Watching close the feet of the lightning fly
Fancy dancers free underneath the sky,
Joining in the circle moving round and round
we come again
to dance again

Chorus

Women shining like the morning sun,
Children making rainbows as they laugh and run,
The old and young meeting like they did long ago
we come again
to dance again

Chorus

David Campbell

Classworks Fiction and Poetry Texts Year 2 © Julie Orrell, Nelson Thornes Ltd 2004

Dragon Dance

Ears alive to every sound,
Clashing cymbal, beating gong,
Fire crackers spinning round,
Happy voices, children's song.

Dragon dance
Dragon leap
Dragon prance.

Dazzled eyes see gold and red,
Weaving streamers, flashing scales,
Mask of flames at dragon's head,
Dancing feet and twisting tails.

Dragon dance
Dragon leap
Dragon prance.

Classworks Fiction and Poetry Texts Year 2 © Julie Orrell, Nelson Thornes Ltd 2004

Diwali

Autumn – darkening season of the year,

Diwali festival is drawing near.

Light now the oil lamp, let it shine out bright,

Casting out shadows of the autumn night.

Darkness of Ravana is far away,

Demon king banished by the lamp's bright ray.

Welcome Rama home with feasting and prayer,

Welcome Lakshmi into homes everywhere.

Autumn – darkening season of the year,

Diwali festival is drawing near.

Text 28

Snake in School

One year in Monsoon season
We all screamed and with good reason:
A water snake had come to school!
But Mister Singh just kept his cool.
He chased him out of our school gate
And told him off for being late!

Debjani Chatterjee

Text 29

A Who'Z Who of the Horrible House

Inside
the
Horrible
House
there is
an awful aquamarine apparition abseiling
a bug-eyed beige bogeyman boxing
a cackling crimson cockroach creeping
a disgusting damson Dracula dancing
an eerie emerald elf electrocuting
a floppy flame Frankenstein fencing
a grotty green ghost groaning
a haunting hazel hag hammering
an insane indigo imp ice-screaming
a jittery jade jackal juggling
a kinky khaki king knitting
a loony lime leprechaun lassooing
a monocled maroon madman marching
a nightmarish navy nastie nipping
an outrageous orange ogre oozing
a phoolish purple phantom phoning
a quadruple quicksilver quagga quaking
a revolting red rattlesnake rock 'n' rolling
a spotty scarlet spectre spitting
a terrible turquoise troll trampolining
an ugly umber uncle umpiring
a violent violet vampire vibrating
a whiskery white werewolf windsurfing
an eXcitable xanthic eXoskeleton eXploding
a yucky yellow yak yelling
a zitty zinc zombie zapping
inside
the
Horrible
House!

Wes Magee

Text 30

The Witch's Brew

Into my pot there now must go
Leg of lamb and a green frog's toe.

Old men's socks and dirty jeans,
A rotten egg and cold baked beans.

Hubble bubble at the double
Cooking pot stir up some trouble.

One dead fly and a wild wasp's sting,
The eye of a sheep and the heart of a King.

A stolen jewel and mouldy salt
And for good flavour a jar of malt.

Hubble bubble at the double
Cooking pot stir up some trouble.

Wing of bird and head of mouse,
Screams and howls from a haunted house.

And don't forget the pint of blood
Or the sardine tin and the clod of mud.

Hubble bubble at the double
Cooking pot stir up some trouble.

Wes Magee

The Owl and the Pussy-Cat

The Owl and the Pussy-Cat went to sea
    In a beautiful pea-green boat,
They took some honey, and plenty of money,
    Wrapped up in a five-pound note.
The Owl looked up to the stars above,
    And sang to a small guitar,
"O lovely Pussy! O Pussy, my love,
    What a beautiful Pussy you are,
        You are,
        You are!
    What a beautiful Pussy you are!"

Pussy said to the Owl, "You elegant fowl!"
    How charmingly sweet you sing!
O let us be married! too long have we tarried:
    But what shall we do for a ring?"
They sailed away, for a year and a day,
    To the land where the Bong-tree grows,
And there in a wood a Piggy-wig stood
    With a ring at the end of his nose,
        His nose,
        His nose,
    With a ring at the end of his nose.

Edward Lear

Text 32

The Owl and the Pussy-Cat (continued)

"Dear Pig, are willing to sell for one shilling
    Your ring?" Said the Piggy, "I will."
So they took it away, and were married next day
    By the Turkey who lives on the hill.
They dined on mince, and slices of quince,
    Which they ate with a runcible spoon;
And hand in hand, on the edge of the sand,
    They danced by the light of the moon,
        The moon,
        The moon,
    They danced by the light of the moon.

Edward Lear

Text 33

From The Jumblies – verse 1

They went to sea in a Sieve, they did,
  In a Sieve they went to sea:
In spite of all their friends could say,
On a winter's morn, on a stormy day,
  In a Sieve they went to sea!
And when the Sieve turned round and round,
And every one cried, "You'll all be drowned!"
They called aloud, "Our Sieve ain't big,
But we don't care a button! We don't care a fig!
  In a Sieve we'll go to sea!"
    Far and few, far and few,
      Are the lands where the Jumblies live:
Their heads are green, and their hands are blue,
      And they went to sea in a Sieve.

Edward Lear

Classworks Fiction and Poetry Texts Year 2 © Julie Orrell, Nelson Thornes Ltd 2004

Text 34

From The Jumblies – verse 4

And all night long they sailed away;
　　And when the sun went down,
They whistled and warbled a moony song
To the echoing sound of a coppery gong,
　　In the shade of the mountains brown.
"O Timballo! How happy we are,
When we live in a sieve and a crockery-jar,
And all night long in the moonlight pale,
We sail away with a pea-green sail,
　　In the shade of the mountains brown!"
　　　Far and few, far and few,
　　　　Are the lands where the Jumblies live;
Their heads are green, and their hands are blue,
　　　And they went to sea in a Sieve.

Edward Lear

Text 35

Ivan and the Firebird

Once upon a time, in the land of the Tsar, there lived a brave young hunter called Ivan. Ivan worked in the court of the Tsar, a foolish and greedy king. Ivan had the good fortune to be the owner of a magic horse. One day, as Ivan was riding through the forest, he spotted a golden feather lying on the ground. It was shining like a ray of sunlight, bright and beautiful. The feather had fallen from the tail of the firebird.

"Do not touch the feather!" warned Ivan's magical horse. "For if you pick up the feather from the tail of a firebird, it will bring you nothing but trouble." Well, Ivan did not fear trouble for he was a brave hunter. He picked up the feather and took it to the Tsar. The Tsar was amazed at the beauty of the golden feather. "Give me the firebird," he demanded, "or you will lose your head!"

Ivan realised that the words of his horse were true. What could he do? He went sadly to his horse and told him of the Tsar's challenge. "Save your tears, master," whinnied the horse, "for your troubles have hardly begun. Go and tell the Tsar that a hundred sacks of corn must be scattered on the field to catch the firebird."

The next morning, as the sun rose, Ivan hid behind a tree. Suddenly, he heard a rustling sound. It was the whispering wings of the firebird. As the beautiful bird flew down to feast on the corn, Ivan trapped it and took it off to the Tsar. Well, the Tsar was well pleased with the gift of the firebird, but he was not satisfied. "Now your task is to fetch me a bride! At the edge of the world, where the golden sun rises above the waves of the sea, lives Princess Vasilisa. Bring her to me, or you will lose your head!"

Ivan went sadly to his horse and told him of the Tsar's challenge. "Save your tears, master," whinnied the horse, "for your troubles have hardly begun. Go and tell the Tsar that you now have need of a tent with a golden roof and food enough for the journey." So Ivan rode upon his magical horse to the land of the rising sun at the edge of the world. As he stepped onto the burning sands, he saw Princess Vasilisa rowing towards the shore in a boat of gold. Ivan pitched his golden tent on the grasslands, prepared food and wine and waited for the princess.

Ivan and the Firebird (continued)

"Princess, I ask you to join me to feast on the fine food of the Tsar," begged Ivan. The princess feasted well and soon became sleepy. Ivan bundled the princess onto the saddle of his horse and sped off back to the Tsar.

The Tsar was well pleased and rewarded Ivan with gifts of gold and silver. But Princess Vasilisa wept silent tears at the thought of marrying the Tsar.

"I can never marry but in my wedding gown, and that is under a secret stone beneath the waves," she cried. Now, the Tsar knew just how clever Ivan was at bringing him all he desired so he sent for Ivan and told him to fetch the gown or lose his head.

"Save your tears, master," whinnied the horse, "for your troubles have hardly begun. Climb on my back."

Together, they raced to the sea. Stepping onto the golden sands, the horse trod on the king of all the crabs. "Please do not harm me, I will grant you whatever you wish," pleaded the giant crab. Ivan told the crab to bring him the gown of Princess Vasilisa, with which the crab summoned thousands of tiny crabs from the waves and sent them down to the secret stone. They soon returned bearing the gown. When the Tsar received the gown he again asked the princess to marry him.

"I will marry you," she replied, "if you tell Ivan to jump into a cauldron of boiling water." Ivan pleaded with the Tsar to let him bid farewell to his trusted horse. Ivan wrapped his arms around the creature's neck and told him of his fate.

"Save your tears, master," whinnied the horse, "for there are worse troubles than this," and he wove a spell web around Ivan, to protect him from the water. When Ivan was thrown into the water, he emerged stronger than ever! As soon as the Tsar saw what had happened to Ivan, he too jumped in, but without the spell was burned by the water.

Ivan became king in the place of the greedy Tsar and soon Ivan and Princess Vasilisa were married. Together with their trusted friend, the magical horse, they lived happily ever after.

Traditional Russian story

The Fisherman and the Greedy Wife

Once upon a time there lived a fisherman. He lived with his wife in a tumbledown pigsty by the sea. The sty had a roof of straw and the wind and rain crept in through the holes in the roof. Every day, the fisherman walked down to the sea to fish while his wife stayed behind to mind the pigs.

One fine morning the fisherman was sitting on a rock fishing with his line. Suddenly, with a tug, his line disappeared down into the depths. The fisherman knew that he must have caught something very big. He reeled in his line and stared with amazement. For there on the end of the line was the biggest flounder he had ever seen. The flounder stared at the fisherman and spoke, "Please do not kill me. I am not really a flounder, but an enchanted prince. Throw me back, throw me back." Well, the fisherman had never heard a fish talk before and he was so surprised that he threw it straight back into the salty sea.

Later that day the fisherman returned home and told his wife the strange tale of the talking fish. "Well, what did you ask for your reward?" demanded his wife.

"I asked for no reward," replied the fisherman. "What more could I wish for?"

"Go straight back now," shouted his wife, "and ask for somewhere better to live than this sty!" So the fisherman trudged back to the water's edge and called out,

"Flounder, flounder, in the sea,
  Grant my wife a wish for me."

The flounder rose up out of the waves and asked, "What does she want?"

The fisherman told the giant fish that his wife wanted to live in a cottage.

"So be it," answered the fish. "She has it already."

When the fisherman arrived home, he found his wife standing to welcome him back to a pretty cottage. For a while, they lived happily in their little cottage until one day the wife decided that they should have asked for a bigger and better wish. She sent the fisherman back to the sea to ask for... a castle! When the fisherman reached the shore the sea was dark and foaming, but again the flounder leapt up and granted her wish.

"So be it," spoke the fish. "She has it already."

The Fisherman and the Greedy Wife
(continued)

Later that day when he returned home, the fisherman saw his wife climbing steps to an enormous stone castle. The floors were crafted of marble and the furniture of gold. Surely this must be enough, the fisherman thought. But the very next morning, his wife stood at the window and exclaimed, "What use is it to live in a castle, if you are not monarch of all you survey? Go and demand that I be queen!"

The fisherman trudged back to the sea, and this time the waves were grey and menacing. "What does your wife want now?" asked the flounder.
"She… wants to be queen!" replied the fisherman.
"So be it," spoke the fish. "She has it already."

The fisherman sloped sadly home to find his wife sitting on a jewel-encrusted throne and wearing a golden crown. This must be the end of it, whispered the fisherman to himself. But it was not. All night, as the fisherman slept, his wife tossed and turned in her four poster bed. What should she have wished for instead? By the morning, she had the answer. "I want to be GOD," she shouted.

With a heavy heart, the fisherman ran down to the sea. At the shore, a violent storm was raging. Lightning flashed, waves crashed and the sky was red with anger. The fisherman shouted over the rage of the wind,

"Flounder, flounder in the sea,
  Grant my wife a wish for me."

"What does she want now?" asked the flounder, tossing in the waves.
"She wants to be God," muttered the fisherman.
"Return to your wife," replied the flounder. "You will find her living in a pigsty."
And there they stayed, from that day to this. The fisherman and his greedy wife.

A traditional tale from Germany

Text 39

Lutey and the Mermaid
Story beginning

Long ago, in the days when the world was far younger than it is today, there lived an old Cornishman called Lutey. He lived with his wife and faithful dog, Jack, in an old granite cottage by the sea. Lutey had fished the waters of Cornwall's rocky coast for half a lifetime, as his father and grandfather had done before him.

But Lutey was not happy with his lot, for the winds and waves often stopped him from venturing out to fish. "My father did tell of days when the sea was so heavy with fish that all he 'ad to do was drop 'is net over the boat and 'twould pull up, laden with gleaming fish. Mackerel, pilchards and all the gifts of the sea."

"Get on with you," scolded his wife, sending him out, with Jack the dog yapping at his heels, "for all the sweeping and cooking is still to be done. Go and see what the tide has washed in."

Classworks Fiction and Poetry Texts Year 2 © Julie Orrell, Nelson Thornes Ltd 2004

Lutey and the Mermaid
Story build-up

As he trudged slowly along the shoreline, kicking the long, black tresses of seaweed, Jack circled his master. As they walked, Jack disappeared from sight to explore the pools left by the morning tide.

"Jack, 'ere boy," called Lutey, scanning the limpet-lined rocks for the little dog.

Suddenly, Lutey heard a loud yelp and, quickly rounding a rock, he found the little dog crouched low on the sand. Before him, in the rockpool, sat a beautiful woman with hair as golden as the morning sun. A tail of silver scales curled onto the rock and the air was filled with a strange singing. Well, old Lutey had never seen a mermaid before, but he had heard tell of sea sirens in tales of old.

"Uh… who… what are you?" whispered Lutey.

"I need your help," the mermaid replied, "for I have been left here by the salty tide and I must return to my children under the sea. If you carry me back, then I will promise you a golden comb that will change your life for ever."

What should he do? Lutey remembered the pew in the old church at Zennor, telling the sad tale of Mathew Trewhella. But if he left her here, she would surely perish along with her children. Rolling up his sleeves, Lutey picked up the strange creature and headed for the sea.

Classworks Fiction and Poetry Texts Year 2 © Julie Orrell, Nelson Thornes Ltd 2004

Text 41

Lutey and the Mermaid
Story problem

Lutey waded in, ready to release the mermaid in the turquoise shallows.

"Deeper, deeper," called the mermaid, "for I cannot swim in sea so shallow." Deeper went Lutey, until waves lapped around his middle. He bent down to lower the mermaid into the sea but again she called, "Deeper, deeper."

When the deepest water reached his shoulders, he tried to release the creature's hands from around his neck.

"Deeper, deeper, come with me," she demanded, "for what is there to keep you in the world of men? I will show you palaces of coral and rock, hidden deep in forests of seaweed. You could be king of all this!"

Lutey stared out to sea, his mind confused. He thought of the promises of the mermaid and was just about to walk further into the waves, when a sudden noise startled him. The bark of the little dog on the shoreline shook him into reason. He cast off the arms of the mermaid and wandered back to shore, not daring to look back once.

Classworks Fiction and Poetry Texts Year 2 © Julie Orrell, Nelson Thornes Ltd 2004

Text 42

Lutey and the Mermaid
Story resolution and ending

He reached the cottage soaked with spray, and breathless. The mermaid kept her word, as mermaids sometimes do. For the next morning, as he walked the shoreline, he found a comb of gold sparkling in the sand. Lutey remembered the words of the mermaid and went to wash the sand off the comb in the waves. To his surprise, the waves calmed to a ripple.

From that day to this, whenever the seas were too wild for fishing, old Lutey leant over the sides of his little wooden boat and combed the waves to stillness. His nets glistened with silver fish and Lutey led a long and happy life.

"I am the happiest man alive... what more could any man ask for?"

Text 43

In the middle of the night

A long time after bedtime
when it's very very late
when even dogs dream
and there's deep sleep
breathing through the house

when the doors are locked
and the curtains drawn
and the shops are dark
and the last train's gone
and there's no more traffic
in the street
because everyone's asleep

then

the window-cleaner comes
to the high-street shop fronts
and shines at the glass
in the street-lit dark

and a dust-cart rumbles past
on its way to the dump
loaded with the last
of the old day's rubbish.

. . .

Kathy Henderson

In the middle of the night (continued)

At the bakery
the bakers in their floury clothes
mix dough in machines
for tomorrow's loaves of bread

and out by the gate
rows of parked vans wait
for their drivers to come
and take the newly-baked
bread to the shops
for the time when the
bread-eaters wake.

. . .

And the mother
with the wakeful child in her arms
walking up and down
and up and down
and up and down
the room
hears the train as it passes by
and the cats by the bins
and the night owl's flight
and hums hushabye and hushabye
we should be asleep now
you and I
it's late and time to close your eyes

it's the middle of the night.

Kathy Henderson

The little boat

Down by the shore
where the sea meets the land,
licking at the pebbles
sucking at the sand,
and the wind flaps
and sunshades
and the ice-cream man
out-shouts the seagulls
and the people come
with buckets and spades
and suntan lotion
to play on the shore
by the edge of the ocean,
a little boy
made himself a boat
from an old piece of
polystyrene plastic,
with a stick for a mast
and a string tail sail
and he splashed
and he played
with the boat he'd made
digging it a harbour
scooping it a creek,
all day long by the edge
of the sea
singing
'We are unsinkable
my boat and me!'

And the boat
sailed out
in the skim of the wind
past the fishermen
sitting on the end of the pier,
out and out
past a crab boat trailing
a row of floats
and a dinghy sailing
a zig-zag track
across the wind,

out where the lighthouse
beam beats by
where the sea birds wheel
in the sky and dive
for the silvery fish
just beneath the waves,
out sailed the little boat
out and away.

...

Kathy Henderson

The little boat (continued)

And the further it sailed
the bigger grew
the ocean
until all around
was sea
and not a sign of land,
not a leaf,
not a bird,
not a sound,
just the wind
and heaving sliding
gliding breathing water
under endless sky.

And then suddenly
up from underneath
with a thrust and a leap
and a mouth full of teeth
came a great fish snapping
for something to eat,
and it grabbed the boat
and dived
deep
deep
deep
down

to where the light grows dim
in the depths of the sea,
a world of fins and claws
and slippery things
and rocks and wrecks
of ancient ships
and ocean creatures
no one's seen.

And there at the shore
where the sea greets the land
licking at the pebbles
sucking at the sand,
a child was standing
she stretched out her hand
and picked up the boat
from the waves at her feet
and all day long
she splashed and she played
with the boat she'd found
at the edge of the sea,
singing
*'We are unsinkable
my boat and me!'*

Kathy Henderson

Have You Ever...? *and* Spellbound

Have You Ever...?

Have you ever...
Climbed the pole at the North Pole?
Read a book you couldn't read?
Seen a mole upon a mole?
Used pencil lead to draw a lead?

Seen a saw – I saw it saw!
Cried a tear about a tear?
Munched a core right to the core?
Fed a bear you couldn't bear?

Seen a school of fish at school?
A match play football at a match?
Played pool in the swimming pool?
Undone a catch to catch a rat?

You need to read and when you've read,
To use the clues inside your head!
They're spelt the same, you can't use sight,
Your brain must tell you which one's right...

Spellbound

I have a spelling chequer
It came with my PC
It plainly marks four my revue
Miss takes I cannot sea.
I've run this poem threw it
I'm shore your pleased too no;
It's letter perfect in it's weigh
My chequer tolled me sew.

Norman Vandal

Sunday in the Yarm Fard

The mat keowed
The mow cooed
The bog darked
The kidgeon pooed

The squicken chalked
The surds bang
The kwuck dacked
The burch rells chang

And then, after all the dacking and changing
The chalking and banging
The darking and pooing
The keowing and the kooing
There was a mewtiful beaumont
Of queace and pie-ate

Trevor Millum

Charlie and the Chocolate Factory
Mr Willy Wonka's Factory

In the evenings, after he had finished his supper of watery cabbage soup, Charlie always went into the room of his four grandparents to listen to their stories, and then afterwards to say good night.

Every one of these old people was over ninety. They were as shrivelled as prunes, and as bony as skeletons, and throughout the day, until Charlie made his appearance, they lay huddled in their one bed, two at either end, with nightcaps on to keep their heads warm, dozing the time away with nothing to do. But as soon as they heard the door opening, and heard Charlie's voice saying, "Good evening, Grandpa Joe and Grandma Josephine, and Grandpa George and Grandma Georgina," then all four of them would suddenly sit up, and their old wrinkled faces would light up with smiles of pleasure – and the talking would begin. For they loved this little boy. He was the only bright thing in their lives, and his evening visits were something they looked forward to all day long. Often, Charlie's mother and father would come in as well, and stand by the door, listening to the stories that the old people told; and thus, for perhaps half an hour every night, this room would become a happy place, and the whole family would forget that it was hungry and poor.

Roald Dahl

Text 50

James and the Giant Peach

Their names were Aunt Sponge and Aunt Spiker, and I am sorry to say that they were both really horrible people. They were selfish and lazy and cruel, and right from the beginning they started beating poor James for almost no reason at all. They never called him by his real name, but always referred to him as "you disgusting little beast" or "you filthy nuisance" or "you miserable creature", and they certainly never gave him any toys to play with or any picture books to look at. His room was as bare as a prison cell.

They lived – Aunt Sponge, Aunt Spiker and now James as well – in a queer ramshackle house on the top of a high hill in the south of England. The hill was so high that from almost anywhere in the garden James could look down and see for miles and miles across a marvellous landscape of woods and fields; and on a very clear day, if he looked in the right direction, he could see a tiny grey dot far away on the horizon, which was the house that he used to live in with his beloved mother and father. And just beyond that, he could see the ocean itself – a long thin streak of blackish-blue, like a line of ink, beneath the rim of the sky.

Roald Dahl

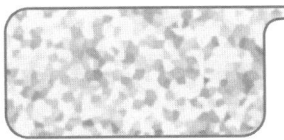

Teaching notes and ideas

Narrative 1

Stories with familiar settings

1–4 Lost in the Supermarket

The story divides into a four-part structure which could be represented pictorially as a storyboard planner to plan children's own versions.

1 Lost in the Supermarket: story opening

Talk with the class about the experience of getting lost and how this makes you feel. **T6**, **T10**

Discuss how the scene is set by introducing the characters straight away. The author appeals to the reader's senses by describing the smell of bread baking. Discuss favourite smells and how they make you feel.

2 Lost in the Supermarket: story build-up

Look at the order in which Joe and his Mum are going around the supermarket. The connectives to signal time help us to get the order right. Can the children draw a map to show the journey through the aisles in the correct order? Highlight how important the connectives are in helping to do this. **T4**, **T11**, **S2**

3 Lost in the Supermarket: story problem

Consider how the author has used detail about Joe's comic to engage the reader. Play 'Improve' (*Developing Early Writing* page 130) as human sentences, starting with a simple sentence 'Joe chose a comic' and adding detail on whiteboards to improve the sentence. Identify all the words used instead of 'went' to describe how Joe travelled when he was looking for Mum. What happens to these words as the problem unfolds? Make a bank of words to use instead of 'went'. Using the device of asking short questions to show Joe's rising panic, generate lots of short, sharp, panic questions and discuss how they might be articulated. **T6**

4 Lost in the Supermarket: story resolution and ending

Encourage children to use their voices with expression to capture the different voices of Joe, the security guard and the woman on the tannoy. Identify the moral contained within the story. **T5**

5–6 The Big Big Sea

Consider how the author starts this story with speech. Starting a story with speech is a device used by many authors as it immediately throws the reader into the action. The story is written as if the little boy is telling us what happened, rather than writing it down. This is a useful text to discuss differences between spoken and written language. Investigate how often the author uses the word 'and' to join phrases and start sentences – why? Explain that when we write stories, we try to use different, interesting connectives, rather than just 'and', but in this story, the author is deliberately using the word to make it sound more like speech. **T3**, **T6**

Consider the use of ellipsis and then capital letters to show what an impact the moon made on the little boy. Support the children in using this structure to identify something powerful at the start of their own stories about a powerful memory for them. The story ending of 'I'll always remember...' makes a good model for writing. **T10**

Poetry

Poems with familiar settings

7 What Is a Million?

Identify the two main text structure features of the poem – the rhyme pattern on lines 2 and 4 of each verse and the word 'The' at the start of lines 1 and 3 of each verse. Generate a class list of things that have huge numbers, to answer the question 'What is a million?' Discuss how the poem is written in the second person: the poet always uses 'you' and doesn't mix it up with 'me' or 'he'. Introduce agreement by rewriting a verse of the poem using 'I' and 'my' to explain the difference. Model and support children in writing their own 'What Is a Million?' poems. **T7, T12**

8 Back to School

Discuss with the children what is new about being in Year 2. Compile a class list of differences writing suggestions vertically as a list. The poet has used a list of new things to make a list poem. Investigate with the children how there are no connectives at the start of lines but simply the items. Point out that the items are separated by commas and introduce the idea of commas (Ref: *Developing Early Writing* Unit G page 142). Allow lots of opportunity to practise reading using commas. Explore the rhyme pattern and identify the rhymes on alternate lines. Count the number of times the word 'new' repeats, the repetition gives a rhythm to the poem. Compose class, group or individual poems about their new school year using key features identified to support. **S3, T12**

9 Playground Rap

This poem would be fun to perform as a speaking and listening outcome. Raps rely heavily on the rhythm of the poem. Investigate the rhythm by chanting the poem out loud, swaying arms or body to the beat. Identify that the rhythm of this poem works on a 4/4 beat line followed by a 9 beat line. In the 4/4 beat lines, the stress comes on the second and fourth syllables (we <u>like</u> to <u>slide</u>, we <u>like</u> to <u>hide</u>) which gives us the rap rhythm. Create a new class rap by discussing things that the class like doing and fitting them into the rhythm. In this particular poem the 9 beat line repeats throughout. **T7**

10 The Monster in my Bedroom

Ask the children to visualise the monster from reading the first two verses. Develop speaking skills in paired talk as the children describe their monster to each other, including lots of blood-thirsty detail. Develop listening skills by challenging the pairs to draw a picture of their partner's monster by listening carefully to their description. Share-read the final verse of the poem and solve the monster mystery. Discuss the humour of the poem.

Notice how the poet has used the pronoun 'it' to reinforce the 'monsterness' factor, whereas in the final verse when the reader discovers the truth, the pronoun changes to 'he'. The rhymes at the end of lines 2 and 4 in each verse provide investigation of the long vowel phonemes /i_e/, /or/ and /ee/. The poem would work well as a poem for presentation as it lends itself to sound effects and drama. **S3, T1, W1, W2**

11 Hector the Collector

Another example of a poem that contains items separated by commas. (*Developing Early Writing* Unit G page 142). **S3**

Narrative 2

Stories

12–15 The First Day of the Holidays

This text supports *Developing Early Writing* Unit 10. This story has clearly identifiable features in common with *Lost in the Supermarket*. As the story is being read, discussed and own versions written, draw attention to the similarities of use of speech, emotions of being lost, a 'suddenly' moment, kind character rescue and moral ending as key similar features. The story divides into a four-part structure which could be represented pictorially as a storyboard planner to plan children's own versions.

12 The First Day of the Holidays: story opening

Investigate how the author sets the scene on the first page. How is the reader given details of 'when', 'where', 'who' and 'what'? The author uses capital letters for the second sentence in order to jolt the reader and make them take notice of how Tegan is feeling. Hold a discussion on how the class feels at the start of an exciting holiday and list suggestions. In the story the image of steam in a kettle is used to describe excitement. What other images could be used instead? **T6, T10**

13 The First Day of the Holidays: story build-up

Collect all the examples on this page of connectives to signal time: 'a few minutes later…', 'after a short while…', 'all morning…' and 'later…' Build up a class bank of connectives to signal time for use in writing story build-ups. **S2, T4**

14 The First Day of the Holidays: story problem

Discuss the dangers of being alone on a beach. Apply these concepts to a familiar setting in your own locality. Consider how the author repeats the phrase 'It was Sam…' to draw you into the situation. This is developed in the use of questions to highlight the dilemma. Explore the use of a 'suddenly' moment for suspense. Discuss and create your own 'suddenly' suspense moments in story problems. **T11**

15 The First Day of the Holidays: story resolution and ending

Explore the use of speech to resolve the problem. Consider how important the adverb 'gently' is in describing the lifeguard's actions, try replacing it with, for example, 'roughly' and see how an adverb can alter the whole feel of a sentence. Identify the moral in the story. **T5**

TERM 2

Narrative 1

Traditional stories

16–19 The Whisp of Straw, the Piece of Coal and the Little Bean

A traditional tale originally told by the Brothers Grimm (refer to the *Classworks Literacy Year 2* unit on 'Traditional tales' pages 99–113 for background information on traditional stories). The tale explains how broad beans have a seam down the middle.

16 The Whisp of Straw, etc: story opening

Identify the type of story that this is likely to be from the opening language, 'Long, long ago...'. Discuss what we already know about traditional tales and make a collection of other traditional stories. **T3**, **W3** (digraph 'wh' in whisp)

Explore the author's use of alliteration in 'bowlful of bouncy broad beans'. Discuss and make observational drawings of vegetables, pointing out their unusual features. Ask the children to choose a vegetable with a distinctive feature which they would like to star in their own tale, for example, potatoes with eyes, dimpled peas or bumpy turnips. Model and support in writing new story beginnings, using a different vegetable. **T13**

17 The Whisp of Straw, etc: story build-up

Explain to the children how the author is using speech to move the action on. Use *Developing Early Writing* Unit E (page 140) to investigate speech marks. Help the class to recognise that the 'traditional' speech repeats in 'Well, my friends.' Act out the scenario between the three companions to develop the conversation before writing own versions. **T7**, **S2**

18 The Whisp of Straw, etc: story problem

Revise the use of time connectives ('before long', 'after a while', 'next') from Year 2 Term 1. Explore with the class examples of onomatopoeia ('crackling', 'sizzling') and model and support use of sound in composition. **T9**

19 The Whisp of Straw, etc: story resolution and ending

Discuss with the children how, because traditional tales were originally spoken and not written, they tend to have more colloquial language than written tales. Collect any traditional words, phrases or expressions from your local area or from a local cultural group. If possible, invite in a local storyteller or willing local grandparent to tell a relevant traditional tale. Finish own stories with an explanation of how the vegetable got its distinctive feature. **T7**

20–23 The Wishing Stone

Huge standing stones are to be found in many parts of Britain. Tales surrounding these stones have been told for centuries by local people and many believe that these ancient stones have magical powers. Useful outcomes for this unit would be acted or spoken (tape recorded) versions of the tale and comparative character profiles to describe Matt at the beginning and the end of the story. **T7**, **T14**

20 The Wishing Stone: story opening

Explore the way that the author sets the scene. Identify the traditional language and the figurative language used in description. Using the first few sentences as a model, ask the children to talk in pairs and decide on a description for an old farmer that really paints a picture for the reader. **T5**

Build up a character profile for the farmer, drawing on the evidence given in the text. **T6**, **T14**

21 The Wishing Stone: story build-up

Working in small groups, ask the class to work on acting out the second section of the story. Try using a commentator to describe Matt's thoughts and feelings or adding voice or music to create an atmosphere. **T7**

22 The Wishing Stone: story problem

Discuss with the class how Matt's character flaw is his downfall. Develop the idea of greedy wishes (common in traditional tales) through the drama. Challenge each group to predict an ending for the tale and to present it to the class. **T4**

Use the text to prompt an investigation of compound words (wheelbarrow). **W4**

23 The Wishing Stone: story resolution and ending

Present the tale for an audience, perhaps another class or for parents. Discuss with the children how Matt's character has changed by the end of the tale – review earlier character profiles and write a new version for the reformed character. **T6**

Poetry

Other cultures

24 Steel Band Jump Up

This poem has a very infectious style, it makes you want to join in! The poet achieves this by using a powerful combination of rhyming couplets, rhythm and repeating refrain. Use this poem with the children to explore these features and link the literacy with music and PE in a performance using music and movement. The children could attempt a new class version, using the key features. **T8, T9, T10, S2**

25 The Pow-wow Drum

This poem has a clear pattern, working on two rhyming lines, one further line to elaborate on the first two lines and then a repeating verse ending and chorus. It was written by a modern poet, recalling and celebrating the customs of the past.
Model for the children how a repeating chorus gives pattern to a poem, using a drum or tambour to beat the rhythm of the words. Compose in shared and guided writing a new verse for the poem using the pattern identified. Ask the class to compare this poem with *Steel Band Jump Up*, discussing which poem they prefer and why. **T15, T11**

26 Dragon Dance

The festival of Chinese New Year falls in Term 2. This poem is a celebration of the sights and sounds of the dragon dance. Explore with the children how the first verse captures the sounds of the dance, whereas the second verse captures the sights. The poem appeals to the senses to transport the listener to the dance. Model and support the class in writing their own poems to capture the sights and sounds of a festival. The rhyme pattern of ABAB differs from the previous two poems, each of which has used a different rhyme structure. Collect an on-going class list of poems that use this structure. **T15**

27 Diwali

A further poem that celebrates a festival (although this time it does not fall in this term), again with a predictable rhyme pattern. Explore with the children the AABBCCDD rhyme pattern and link to other poems that use this pattern. In this poem the last two lines echo the first two lines, making the poem complete. Investigate how the /ie/ phoneme is represented in 'bright' and 'night' as 'igh' and generate a list of words containing an /ie/ sound that use this spelling pattern (REF: *Progression in Phonics* Step 7 – Rhyme generation and word sort game). **W1, T9**

28 Snake in School

A modern poem from India by Debjani Chatterjee which tells the tale of the day a snake came to school. Use this poem as a model for writing a new poem about the day something unusual happened in your own school. Discuss with the class how in India it would not be unusual to see a snake. Research snakes in the school library and identify snakes found in Britain and those snakes not found in Britain, drawing them in two sets with captions. The poem itself provides a good framework for a new poem, for example:

The day a grass snake came to school
Mrs Bray just kept her cool.
She chased him out of our school gate
And told him off for being late!

Higher achieving pupils could use the rhyme pairs 'school/cool' and 'gate/late' to write an independent four line poem. **T15**

Poems by significant children's poets

29 A Who'Z Who of the Horrible House

This alphabet poem by Wes Magee provides a creative opportunity to explore alphabetical order through a poem. Using the starting lines of 'Inside the Horrible House there is...', challenge the class to work in pairs to work on one letter each and use a dictionary to research unusual words for their letter. Explore with the class how each line works on the pattern of adjective, adjective, noun, verb, highlighting these in three different colours on the shared text. Discuss what role adjectives, nouns and verbs play in a sentence. Ask each pair to refine their list of possible words so that they are left with only two adjectives, a noun and a verb that fit together to make a silly sentence for their letter. Discuss how the poet presents the poem visually. Assemble the new class poem in alphabetical order. **S7, T15**

30 The Witch's Brew

In this poem Wes Magee again uses unusual (and revolting!) items but in a different format. Identify the rhyming couplets and link back to other poems you have discussed that use this pattern. The repeating chorus would provide a refrain to link new pairs of rhyming lines. **T9**

31–32 The Owl and the Pussy-Cat

Research with the class who Edward Lear was, and when he lived. Discuss the concept of a nonsense poem, this concept will be developed in Term 3 through reading poems with language play. This example provides a good model for exploring unusual vocabulary, as many of the words are old words that the children will not have come across before ('elegant', 'fowl', 'charmingly', 'tarried', 'shilling', 'quince' and 'runcible'). Demonstrate how to break unfamiliar words down into syllables ('runcible', 'elegant'). Challenge the class to highlight on a copy of the text any words that they do not understand and to work in pairs to use the context of the poem to take a guess at what they might mean. Some words have almost completely dropped out of usage, such as shilling – discuss with the class how our language is constantly evolving. Work as a class to write a shared modern-day class version of *The Owl and the Pussy-Cat*. **W5, W10, T12**

33–34 *From* The Jumblies

Edward Lear also wrote this classic poem. Work with the class to extend previous work on unusual vocabulary to explore unusual phrases and expressions ('we don't care a button, we don't care a fig', 'O Timballo', etc.), and discuss how the children's great or great-great grandparents would have used very different expressions to those used today. The poem also invites the reader to picture the lands where the Jumblies live – the poet creates a mystical air through his choice of words ('shade', 'coppery', 'moonlight', 'echoing', 'moony song') yet doesn't actually describe the lands. Model for the class how you are going to use these clues to help you imagine what the lands are like and write a description of the lands where the Jumblies live. Challenge the class to write their own descriptions. Make a three dimensional class display of the lands where the Jumblies live and display children's descriptions around it. **W10, T15**

Narrative 2

Traditional stories from other cultures

35–36 Ivan and the Firebird

Recap with the class work on traditional tales earlier in the term. Make a class poster of all the features that you can remember of a traditional tale and add to this as a checklist as the unit develops. Read the Russian tale of *Ivan and the Firebird* and identify what makes it a traditional tale. Discuss how we can place this as a Russian tale because of the cultural differences from a British tale (names, Tsar, grasslands). Explain to the class that although the tale comes from a different culture, it has elements in common with more familiar traditional tales. Find Russia on the globe and look in library books to find out about customs. Explore features of the tale at word, sentence and text level, including alliteration, unusual words (Tsar, names), figurative language, speech, story language, repeating refrain from the horse, magical creature, unheeded warning, repeated challenge, granted wish, happy ending. Model how to write the story in an extended nine-part 'story mountain' structure of beginning, event, warning, problem 1, problem 2, problem 3 (including a wish), problem 4, resolution and story ending. Support the children in making their own zig-zag books with nine pages to represent the nine sections, each with a picture and caption underneath to show what is happening in the tale. **S6, T1, T3, T15**

37–38 The Fisherman and the Greedy Wife

This traditional tale comes from Germany and exploits the theme of a repeated wish ending in the greedy pair being put back where they had started. Refer back to the same device used in *The Wishing Stone* (Texts 20–23). This traditional tale makes a good model for writing.

39–42 Lutey and the Mermaid

Fabulous creatures such as mermaids have long been the subject of traditional tales. This Cornish tale uses a classic 'story mountain' structure. Explore with the class key features at text, sentence and word level, including: traditional tale language; setting; character; dialect speech; connectives to show time; powerful verbs; happy ending. Act out the tale, developing the role of speech and model writing a new version of the mermaid tale. **S6**

The pew referred to in the story is found in Zennor church. It commemorates Mathew Trewella who, according to the legend, was lured into the sea by the beautiful mermaid, Morveren.

TERM 3

Narrative 1

Different stories by the same author

43–46 In the middle of the night *and* The little boat

These lyrical stories by Kathy Henderson have a very powerful rhythm from the repeating words and phrases, choice of vocabulary and lack of punctuation. They are poem-like in presentation. Compare similarities and differences between the two.

43–44 In the middle of the night

Investigate the device by which the author repeats the 'when...' clauses at the start of the story – 'when it's very, very late' gives us the basic information yet the next two add much more detail. Using whiteboards, encourage the children to try their own 'when...' sequences. Challenge the children to identify which word the author uses next for the same device.

This story is unusual as it does not have a clear 'story mountain' structure, but works rather as a series of little video clips of what is going on in different parts of the city in the middle of the night. The text lends itself to a class story, with children contributing snapshot night-time sequences to assemble into a whole. Draw up a checklist with the class of the key features identified, to ensure that it all fits together well: lack of punctuation, repeating connectives, repeating night-time words ('night', 'sleep', 'asleep', 'dark', 'light') and short phrases on separate lines, like a poem. **S1**

45–46 The little boat

Although the style of language and sentence is similar to the previous story, the structure differs. In this story, the author tells a chronological tale of the voyage of the little boat, whereas in *In the middle of the night* the story was organised into cameos. Explore with the class key features of the text, such as story round, descriptive story start, repeating 'not a...' phrase, use of the word 'and' to push the story along, punctuation, figurative language. Model how you are going to write a sustained story, describing the boat's journey and using the style and structure of the text as a model. Support the children in writing their own sustained independent stories as the unit builds. **T4, T10**

Poetry

Texts with language play

47 Have You Ever...? *and* Spellbound

Have You Ever...?: Discuss with the class how certain words may sound the same, but be spelt differently and have very different meanings whereas other words have the same spelling, but can mean different things.

Identify that both poets are playing with words in these examples of poems. In word level work, explore words that have the same spelling but can mean different things (homographs). Discuss how with these words we have to use the context of the sentence to make sense of the word. Draw up a class list of words that have the same spelling but more than one meaning (for example, 'read', 'lead', 'pool', 'cool'). Reflect in guided reading. Compile on-going class charts for words spelt the same with two meanings and for words that sound the same but have different spellings (homographs). Compose a class poem based on language play using *Have You Ever...?* as a model and the class word list as a wordbank. **W6, T11**

Spellbound: Read the poem aloud to the class (but don't look at it!) Discuss what a spell check is. Use the computer to demonstrate how you can check the spelling of a word electronically. Give the class the opportunity to type in familiar words (try their names!) and see which words it rejects. Demonstrate how when the programme doesn't know a word, it suggests other similar spellings instead.

48 Sunday in the Yarm Fard

Read the poem with the class and identify that the first sounds of words are being switched around. Explore this as a concept, by using magnetic letters and physically swapping initial sounds to make new nonsense words. Ask the children to try this trick with their own names or the name of the school.

In pairs, children make wordplay puzzles for their partner to solve. Model writing your own poem using this wordplay technique, based on another setting such as the zoo (for example, the hake snissed, the rion loared...). Compose a class list of zoo animals and noises as a wordbank and support the class in writing their own poems. **T8, T11**

Narrative 2

Extended texts by significant children's authors

49 Charlie and the Chocolate Factory

Use the texts *Charlie and the Chocolate Factory* and *James and the Giant Peach* as class stories and investigate aspects of the extended story through this unit of work, leading to a book review.

Reinforce examples of word and sentence level work, for example, in this extract from Chapter 2, Dahl describes the grandparents in Charlie's house. Use the descriptions to role-play the scene. Use hot-seating and ask the children in role to answer a range of questions for the class such as: 'What is your favourite bit of the day?', 'Where do you spend your day?', 'Who is your favourite visitor?'

Model how you can use the information that the author has given us in just one paragraph to answer these questions as statements. In pairs, children act as reporters or interviewees and role-play and record questions and answers. **S6**

Make notes on what you liked about the story.

Research the life of Roald Dahl and make a list or collection of the books he has written. **T5**

50 James and the Giant Peach

Compare this story to another book by Dahl (see Text 49) and discuss preferences. Model and support the class in composing a book review of their favourite Dahl story. **T4, T12**